I0402650

This dotted book belongs to:

____

www.ingramcontent.com/pod-product-compliance
Lightning Source LLC
Chambersburg PA
CBHW060858220526
45466CB00003B/1419
9781701379398